MODERN FIRST EDITIONS: POINTS AND VALUES

(Second Series)

This edition is limited to 1,000 copies.
Copy number...*389*....

MODERN FIRST EDITIONS: POINTS AND VALUES

(Second Series)

BY
GILBERT H. FABES
AND
WILLIAM A. FOYLE

W. and G. Foyle Ltd.
"At the Sign of the Trefoile"
London

Published June 1931

DEDICATED TO
FRANK GLENN
OF KANSAS CITY
BOOKMAN AND GENIAL FRIEND

FOREWORD
BY
WILLIAM A. FOYLE

The success of the first series of *Modern First Editions: Points and Values* proved the necessity for books of practical value for the use of collectors of modern first editions. Only seven hundred and fifty copies of the book were issued and the whole edition was oversubscribed before publication.

It has therefore been decided that a larger edition of the second series is required, and the publishers have thought that the best plan would be to limit the edition to one thousand copies which, though it will enable a larger number of collectors to obtain the book, yet—in fairness to the purchasers—the issue be still kept to a reasonable limit.

In collaborating with Gilbert Fabes, whose knowledge of his subject is possibly unique, I feel that I have, as a bookseller, some satisfaction in knowing that the issuing of books of practical value is a policy which will receive the support of all who are genuinely interested in the distribution of bibliographical information.

Some criticism was expected on the appearance of Mr. Fabes's previous volume. It was asserted that a book giving the points and values of books should not have been published because it gave away too many trade secrets. This is a matter of opinion, but I am definitely in favour of the policy expressed in these books because I believe that the greater the interest aroused in our modern books, the better it will be for all who buy, sell and collect them.

The bookseller of to-day has to realise that in dealing with collectors he is dealing with a class quite capable of discovering for themselves bibliographical facts of importance. Further, many of them are quite capable of treating the matter of collecting in the serious manner it deserves, and they are alert to the changing values, points of issue, and of many other details that have to be learned before they may become good bookmen.

It is, in my opinion, essential that the modern bookseller should realise this, and assist, rather than hinder, the activities of the book collectors.

After all, connoisseurs of most of the other branches of collecting are thoroughly well catered for, and hundreds of books have been written dealing with the values and points of pictures, pottery, etchings, engravings, glass, silver, foreign stamps and so on.

If I wish to know the value of any postage stamp, I need only to buy Messrs. Stanley Gibbon's catalogue and find out.

I know, of course, that I should not receive their catalogued price if I wished to sell, but still, I have the value. Further, such catalogues are full of points—the collector wishes to know these—and does not want to place anything in his collection which is not " right," and would rather pay more for the correct article than buy cheaper and speculatively, and find that he has spent money unwisely.

The same freedom in publishing values is done by most of the other trades dealing with the arts and crafts, and although I would not like it to be thought that I believe that the book trade practises subterfuge to a greater extent than any other, I feel that books of the character of this present volume deserve the welcome and the support they obtain.

Like the Walrus, I would say " The time has come to talk of many things," but in addition to the revered Walrus's remarks, garrulity with a purpose is more opportune at the present time, and instead of cabbages we will discuss those magical, elusive, and fascinating creatures—books.

WILLIAM A. FOYLE.

INTRODUCTION

The pioneer volume of this series, *Modern First Editions: Points and Values*, was published in 1929, and proved an immediate success.

The present volume is a continuation. The gathering together in convenient form of this practical information for the use and benefit of collectors of modern first editions is a task in which I have been assisted by my collaborator, William A. Foyle.

Some criticism and much praise came to me after the publication of the first volume, and the criticisms generally took the line that the values were of little real use, owing to the fluctuations of the market in modern first editions.

In the introduction to that volume I stated "that the prices are subject to fluctuations, and due allowance must be made for this contingency."

Presumably, reviewers and others do not read prefaces!

To the collectors, I must address myself and repeat the warning, and even more emphatically, because the market prices of the modern first editions have undergone a great change during the past two years.

The chief objective of these volumes is not to give the market values of the books listed, but to give the details of the variations which separate the issues of collected books, and the values given must be considered only as a comparative guide.

If, for instance, a volume is priced in its first issue at ten pounds and in the second issue at one pound, it should be accepted that the former is worth ten times as much as the latter, but, at the same time, the attempt has been made to give a fair average value in both cases.

This "fair average value" is a term to be understood. It is the retail price at which the book can be valued, subject to its condition being in the "mint" or "very fine" state, generally desired by the collector. Book values are most elusive, and just how variable they are can be discovered by anyone desirous of experimenting.

As an example, let us assume that a collector wishes to sell a superfine copy of the first issue of *Just So Stories*, and takes it to a dozen different booksellers; the prices offered would all be different! Better still—take the same volume to a dozen different experts and ask them to forecast the price which that volume will bring at auction, and they would all be wrong in their forecast! When the famous manuscript of *Alice in Wonderland* was up for sale, I played this game, and asked quite a dozen of the best bookmen in London their idea of the selling price.

The most optimistic of them was five thousand pounds under the final figure!

Further, it must be understood by collectors

that almost every modern first edition that has been out into the world, and has been handled, suffers from a change in its condition, and obtains an individuality, and must be appraised accordingly.

There are no two copies exactly alike of such a volume as a first edition of *The War of the Worlds*, for instance, and each copy has its own slight differences of condition, due to the damages of time and men.

. . . . .

The modern first edition market has undergone a decided change during the past two years, and prices have fallen considerably, and especially in the case of the premier or higher priced items. This has been caused by the alteration in the economic conditions in this country and in America, and the fact that modern first editions had been accepted as substantial securities against the crash of other markets.

Prices for modern books rose to absurd heights as a result of the intensive buying, and the English booksellers were forced to follow, and in many cases, make the market.

The passing of the year 1930 saw the end of the greatest decade in the history of book collecting, and the effects of the upheaval of prices have not yet been realised by any grade of bookmen.

The future of the modern first edition market requires analysis, but I am confident that the reaction will be favourable, because the progress and the standard of English Literature in this twentieth century have been real and high. . . . J. B. Priestley is compared with Dickens, and A. A. Milne with Lewis Carroll. . . .

Let us consider Galsworthy, Shaw, Kipling, Wells, Barrie and Masefield. Great men of mark. Let us note the lesser men in their dozens, and include such names as Walpole, Belloc, Beerbohm, Chesterton, Noyes, Sassoon, Drinkwater, Huxley, George Moore and . . .

Let us study even the next rank, and analyse the works of A. P. Herbert, Rhys Davies, H. E. Bates, A. E. Coppard, Lytton Strachey, Thomas Burke, H. M. Tomlinson, Edmund Blunden, Walter de la Mare, T. F. Powys, Henry Williamson, Humbert Wolfe . . .

Let us remember the men of the period, since dead. . . . Thomas Hardy, W. H. Hudson, C. E. Montague, Rupert Brooke, Edward Thomas, James Elroy Flecker, Joseph Conrad and D. H. Lawrence.

The answer to the question of the future possibilities and eventual reasonable stability of the modern first edition market is obvious when we consider the undoubted prestige with which all of these writers have surrounded, or are surrounding, English Literature. The unsteadiness of the world markets cannot shake my faith in the soundness of the writers of our time, and in the advantages which present themselves to enable collectors to purchase worthy modern books at prices which are now down to a reasonable and sane level.

Experience has taught us that the highest figure obtained for a book does not fix the value of that book at that figure, and the fall in prices will eventually benefit modern literature and its collectors. The soulless and damaging speculators who caused us to be influenced in our opinions upon the merits of modern books through the high prices paid, will disappear or turn their divided attentions to other things less difficult to understand.

So, too, I hope, will disappear the pseudo " Collected Author," for this gentleman and his publisher have done a great deal of harm to the legitimate and delightful pursuit of modern book collecting. We have had an outpouring of " Collectors' Editions." Many of the volumes have been puerile, ridiculous, and altogether unworthy in substance and ludicrously, but tragically exorbitant in price.

At prices ranging from one to ten guineas we have had limited editions, and editions de luxe, signed by their authors, and printed on hand-made papers, or papers from some special mill, with uncut edges, bound in vellums, shagreens, parchments and so on—and within the covers we find perhaps two or three thousand words or less, deserving only a page or two in a reasonably literary magazine, or a few columns in a high-brow journal with a circulation of one thousand or less.

I regret the fact that certain great authors succumbed to the demand, and though generally it can be said that with the best authors there was no exploitation, there have been obvious exceptions.

To criticise one or more of the books which have been foisted upon a faithful book collecting public would be unfair, but of this offshoot of the modern first edition collecting game, there is no need to say more than to express the wish that publishers and authors will realise that the time for the grand harvest has passed.

The desire for limited editions of the best authors is a legitimate one, and it is unfortunate that many mere scraps of printing should have been so ruthlessly thrust upon the market.

. . . . .

Book collecting is a great and noble game, which gives the utmost satisfaction if the buying is at all times studiously considered, and the adding to one's own bookshelves the correct and desirable first editions of the best authors, repays immediately and for all time the wisdom of one's spending.

It is easy to collect modern books; there are so many thousands published each year, but the selection of those books is a matter calling for a goodly mixture of the virtues which go to the making of the complete book collector.

The modern book collector must have foresight, book sense, individuality of thought, faith, knowledge of values, bibliographical knowledge and many other virtues, and above all he must be a book collector and not a speculator or something between an avowed book dealer and a mere book accumulator. I cannot understand, at the present time, the evident lack of foresight which allows the first editions of John Masefield to rest untouched, and at low prices, upon the shelves of the bookshops. Only let a section of the speculative public begin to collect Masefield intensively and the prices will rise.

Surely Masefield will always be known and remembered as a Poet Laureate who has written many fine pieces which may even become standard works?

Rudyard Kipling and Alfred Noyes too! They are being quietly neglected and for why? Simply because the instinct of the herd actuates very viciously with book collectors in the same manner as in many other walks of life. Let a famous journalist tell the world to-morrow that the books of Benito Binks should be bought, or let a famous statesman give a fillip to his favourite author and the whole (senseless) world of amateur "book collectors" will fly after all of their first editions, irrespective of literary values.

GILBERT H. FABES.

ACKNOWLEDGEMENT

To George Taylor, Bookman, of Charing Cross Road, we tender our thanks.

LASCELLES ABERCROMBIE
EMBLEMS OF LOVE
Cr. 8vo. Green cloth

JOHN LANE

1912

There are two issues of the first edition of this book, the correct first issue being bound in rough green cloth with gilt lettering on the front cover and on the spine, and a gilt emblematic figure on the front cover and on the spine. Top edges gilt, others uncut. The second issue is bound in pale green cloth, with brown lettering and decoration on the front cover. Top edges green, others uncut.

Values: First issue .. 15/-
Second issue .. 7/6

MAURICE BARING

LOST DIARIES

Cr. 8vo

DUCKWORTH AND CO.

1913

The first issue is bound in dark green cloth with gilt lettering on the front cover within an oval of dark blue cloth, and lettered in gilt on spine within an oblong of dark blue cloth. The second issue is bound in light green cloth and lettered in black.

Values: First issue .. £1
Second issue .. 10/-

J. M. BARRIE
AN EDINBURGH ELEVEN

Foolscap 8vo

" BRITISH WEEKLY "

1889

The first issue is bound in white paper wrappers with black and red lettering on front cover.

The second issue is bound in grey cloth, gilt lettered.

Values: First issue .. £6
Second issue .. £5

J. M. BARRIE

SHALL WE JOIN THE LADIES?
AND OTHER
ONE-ACT PLAYS

Cr. 8vo.   Blue cloth

HODDER AND STOUGHTON

1929

On the verso of the title page of the first issue the only lettering is:

"Made and Printed in Great Britain for Hodder and Stoughton Ltd. | by T. and A. Constable, Printers, Edinburgh."

In the second issue of the first edition the words "First Edition . . . July, 1929" have been added to the centre of the verso of the title page, and the title page has been mounted on the stub of the previous title page. (The publishers state that a certain number of copies were inadvertently printed without any date, and these copies have a cancel title, but that they were only part of the first edition.)

Values: First issue .. £2
Second issue .. 15/-

H. E. BATES
CATHERINE FOSTER
Cr. 8vo

JONATHAN CAPE

1929

The first issue is bound in bluish green cloth, and the second issue is bound in grey green cloth.

Values: First issue .. 25/-
Second issue .. 15/-

MAX BEERBOHM

SEVEN MEN

Cr. 8vo.   Blue cloth

WILLIAM HEINEMANN

1919

The first issue is generally supposed to be that bound in " diced " cloth, and the second is bound in straight grain cloth.

Values: First issue   .. £2
         Second issue .. £1

ARNOLD BENNETT

A MAN FROM THE NORTH

Cr. 8vo.   Red cloth

JOHN LANE
1898

The first issue has a twelve page list of advertisements at the end of the volume, dated 1897. A later issue has the advertisements dated 1898.

Values: First issue   .. £10
Second issue .. £5

JOURNALISM FOR WOMEN

Foolscap 8vo.   Blue cloth

JOHN LANE
1898

The first issue is bound in blue cloth with lettering and designs in red and a twelve page catalogue list at end dated 1897.

The second issue has the advertisements dated 1898.

Values: First issue   .. £4
Second issue .. £2

AUGUSTINE BIRRELL
OBITER DICTA

SECOND SERIES

Cr. 8vo.   Green cloth

ELLIOT STOCK
1887

The two issues of the first edition vary in the following particulars:

The first issue has white end papers and two pages of advertisements at the end.

The second issue has black end papers and an errata slip at page (VII) with a note:

Note

The paper on "Pope" was delivered at a lecture in Birmingham before the Midland Institute.

Errata

Page 92, seven lines from top, for "deep" read "sleep".

Page 215, last line, for "see" read "set".

There are no pages of advertisements to the second issue.

Values: First issue .. £1
Second issue .. 10/-

DAVID W. BONE

MERCHANTMEN-AT-ARMS

New edition with introduction by

H. M. TOMLINSON

Demy 8vo. Blue cloth

CHATTO AND WINDUS

1929

This new edition is the first edition with the introduction by H. M. Tomlinson.

A few copies only, probably advance copies for review and travellers' samples, were bound in dark blue buckram.

The second issue is bound in a smoother greenish-blue cloth.

Values: First issue .. £2
Second issue .. 15/-

RUPERT BROOKE
LETTERS FROM AMERICA

Large Cr. 8vo. Black Buckram

SIDGWICK AND JACKSON
1916

The first issue has the date 1915 on the paper title label.

The second issue has the date 1916.

Values: First issue .. £8
Second issue .. £2

THOMAS BURKE
WHISPERING WINDOWS
Cr. 8vo. Cloth

GRANT RICHARDS

1921

The first issue is bound in brown cloth with black lettering; the surface of this cloth is rough, of the linen type. The depth of the book, i.e. the width of the pages including the covers is approximately one inch. The foredges are rough cut.

The second issue is bound in a lighter brown cloth with a smoother surface. The depth of the book is approximately one and a half inches. The foredges are trimmed, the bottom edges being uncut in both issues.

Values: First issue .. 15/-
Second issue .. 7/6

ROY CAMPBELL
ADAMASTOR

Crown 8vo. Bright Red cloth

FABER AND FABER

1930

Surrounding this book is a bright green paper wrapper and the first edition wrapper has the wording, as follows, along the spine:

Roy Campbell (asterisk) Roy Campbell.

The second issue of the wrapper is worded: Adamastor (asterisk) Roy Campbell.

Very few copies of the issue with the incorrect wording on the wrapper, are in circulation, and such copies are comparatively scarce.

Values: With first issue wrapper .. £1

With second issue wrapper .. 10/-

G. K. CHESTERTON
THE BALL AND THE CROSS
Cr. 8vo. Green cloth

WELLS GARDNER DARTON AND CO., LTD.

1910

The first issue has the title page as part of the collation and the second has the title page mounted on a stub.

Values: First issue .. £1
Second issue .. 10/-

MANALIVE
Cr. 8vo

THOMAS NELSON AND SONS

1912

Two issues of this book exist, the accepted first issue being bound in blue cloth, gilt lettered on spine and blind stamped with the title and author's name on the front cover. Decorated end papers.

A different issue is bound in green cloth, gilt lettered on spine, blind tooled front cover, plain end papers.

Values: First issue .. £1
Second issue .. 10/-

G. K. CHESTERTON

ORTHODOXY

Cr. 8vo

THE BODLEY HEAD

1909

Bound in green cloth, gilt lettered, two variant issues may be identified. The first has gilt tops, and other edges uncut and the second has gilt tops and other edges cut. The latter is a trifle smaller than the former.

Values: First issue .. £1
Second issue .. 10/-

A. E. COPPARD

CLORINDA WALKS IN HEAVEN

Cr. 8vo. Yellow boards

GOLDEN COCKEREL PRESS

1922

The first edition was bound as above, and a second edition, often confused with the correct first edition, was published and bears the imprint of Jonathan Cape, Ltd., although the same sheets were apparently used.

Values: First issue .. £6
Second issue .. 10/-

PINK FURNITURE

Cr. 8vo

JONATHAN CAPE

1930

A very puzzling book for the collector of Modern First Editions, and there are at least six variant issues.

The rarest issue was bound in pink cloth, and has the date 1929 on the verso of the title page. This issue was not available through the ordinary channels, and is very rare.

The second issue and the third are bound in pink cloth with the thread of the material being vertical in the one case and horizontal in the other. Possibly the vertical issue is rarer.

The fourth issue is bound in reddish cloth.

The fifth issue is bound in yellow cloth.

The sixth issue is bound in pink cloth similar to that of the second and third issues.

The first five issues have a misprint on page 191, the letter " t " of the word " It's," in the last line but one from the bottom of the page, is upside down, and in the sixth issue the word is correct. This point saves possible confusion between the pink cloth issues, for there are other minor details separating the issues, which are easily discovered upon comparison.

Values:		
First issue	..	£15
Second issue	..	£3
Third issue	..	£3
Fourth issue	..	10/-
Fifth issue	..	7/6
Sixth issue	..	7/6

A. E. COPPARD

THE BLACK DOG
Cr. 8vo.   Green boards
JONATHAN CAPE
1923

The correct first edition of this important item is bound in green boards with black linen back and paper title label, top edges cut, other edges uncut.

It is important to notice that a second " issue " of the first edition of the book has by some mysterious means made its appearance.

The format of this issue is the same as described above, but the points by which the genuine first edition may be distinguished are as follows:

The word " The " of *The Black Dog* on the title page has an inward curl to the lower part of the letter " h," but in the wrong issue this letter has an upward and outward finish. This letter " h " is uniform with the same letter in the word " other " on the title page of the first and correct issue, but is not so in the incorrect issue.

Further, the letter " J " of " Jonathan " at the foot of the title page is well finished with a curl, in the first issue; but in the other issue the letter is shortened and without the semblance of a curl.

A close inspection of the title page will discover that in the later issue the page does not form part of the collation, and a description of the points is here given because many copies of this later issue have come into circulation.

Values: First issue .. £15
Second issue .. £1

S. R. CROCKETT
LAD'S LOVE

Cr. 8vo.   Green cloth

BLISS, SANDS AND CO.
1897

The first edition can be confused with that published in 1902 by Messrs. Hodder and Stoughton, which issue gives no indication of any other, and was presumably printed from the same plates.

Values: First issue .. £1
Second issue .. 5/-

JOHN DAVIDSON

EARL LAVENDER

Cr. 8vo. Blue buckram

WARD AND DOWNEY
1895

The first issue is bound as above, with brown end papers.

The second issue is bound in dark blue cloth, plain end papers.

The full title of the book is:

A Full and True Account of the Wonderful Mission of Earl Lavender, which Lasted One Night and One Day: With a History of the Pursuit of Earl Lavender and Lord Brumm by Mrs. Scamler and Maud Emblem.

A frontispiece by Audrey Beardsley appears in both issues.

Values: First issue .. 30/-
Second issue .. 10/-

WALTER DE LA MARE

WALTER DE LA MARE
MEMOIRS OF A MIDGET
Cr. 8vo.   Blue cloth

W. COLLINS SONS AND CO. LTD.

1921

The first issue has the words " Copyright 1921 " printed on verso of title page.

The second issue has the same words, with the addition of " Printed in Great Britain," at the foot of the same page.

The third issue has the word " Manufactured " instead of " Printed ".

Values: First issue   ..   £3
           Second issue ..   £2
           Third issue   ..   30/-

WALTER DE LA MARE

THE THREE MULLA MULGARS
Crown 8vo. Cloth

DUCKWORTH AND CO.

1910

The first issue is bound in green cloth, lettered on the back and on the front cover, in gilt, with a design in black on the front cover. There is a publishers' device in black on the back cover. Top edges gilt, foredges cut.

The second issue is bound in light green cloth, black lettered on front cover and on the back, and the publishers' device in black on the back cover. All edges cut. Plain top edges.

Values: First issue .. £3
        Second issue .. £1

NORMAN DOUGLAS
OLD CALABRIA

Demy 8vo.   Green cloth

MARTIN SECKER

1915

The first issue has white end papers.

The second issue has a map of Calabria printed in green on the end papers.

Note: Opinions differ upon the priority of the two issues, but Mr. Martin Secker agreed with the order here given.

Values: First issue   .. £8
Second issue .. £4

ERNEST DOWSON
LA FILLE AUX YEUX D'OR

Royal 8vo

LEONARD SMITHERS
1896

The first issue is bound in yellow gold cloth, lettered in brown.

The second issue is issued in purple cloth and lettered in gold.

Values: First issue .. £3
Second issue .. £1

CONAN DOYLE
THE DOINGS OF RAFFLE HAW

Cr. 8vo

CASSELL AND CO.
1892

The first edition is bound as above with gilt lettered title, author's name, and publishers' name on the spine with eight pages of publishers' advertisements at the end.

Another, and misleading issue, giving no indication of the edition was dated 1893 and is bound in blue cloth, with the title and author's name together in a panel on the spine; the publisher's name appearing at the bottom of the spine between two gilt lines. There are sixteen pages of advertisements at the end, dated 5G.8.93 and 5B.8.93.

Values: First issue .. £4

Second issue ... 10/-

JOHN DRINKWATER
CROMWELL AND OTHER POEMS
Cr. 8vo

DAVID NUTT

1913

The first issue is bound in red cloth lettered in gilt, and with gilt top edges.

The second issue is bound in dark blue cloth, lettered in blind on front cover and in gilt on the spine. Plain edges.

Values: First issue .. £2
Second issue .. £1

POEMS OF MEN AND HOURS
Cr. 8vo

DAVID NUTT

1911

The first issue is bound in cream boards, gilt lettered.

The second issue is bound in grey boards lettered in black.

Values: First issue .. £2
Second issue .. £1

LORD DUNSANY
FIFTY POEMS

Cr. 8vo.   Brown cloth

G. P. PUTNAM'S SONS
1929

The first edition, bound as above, was limited to 250 copies, so described on the verso of the title page.

Simultaneously the ordinary edition was published, and bound in blue cloth, but on the verso of the title page the words, " Reprinted October 1929 " are added.

This edition was evidently printed from the same plates, and has the same type area, and it is a debatable point whether such an edition, classed as a " first ordinary edition " as distinct from a " limited edition," should be so detailed, yet undoubtedly part of the first edition here, is a reprint, and the other part is a limited edition.

Values: First (limited) edition .. 10/6
First (ordinary) edition ... 5/-

JAMES ELROY FLECKER
FORTY TWO POEMS

Cr. 8vo.   Dark Red cloth

J. M. DENT AND SONS LTD.

1911

The first issue has gilt top edges.
The second issue has dark red top edges.

Values: First issue .. £2
Second issue .. 15/-

SELECTED POEMS

Small Cr. 8vo

MARTIN SECKER

1918

The first issue is bound in blue cloth, with paper title label on spine reading lengthways, "Selected Poems of J. E. Flecker." There is a sixteen page publisher's catalogue at the end, dated MCMXV.

The second issue is bound in blue boards, with title label as above. At the end of the book is a sixteen page catalogue of books, dated MCMXX.

Values; First issue .. £1
Second issue .. 10/-

JOHN FREEMAN
THE GROVE
AND OTHER POEMS
Cr. 8vo. Blue cloth

SELWYN AND BLOUNT

1924

The first issue was withdrawn owing to an error in the first line of the poem " The Caliphs."

In this issue the line :

" Caliphs in endless twilight telling again "

appears as the first line of the first verse and also as the first line of the second verse.

In the second issue the first line of the first verse is altered to:

" Caliphs reclining upon lemon moons."

Values: First issue .. £3
         Second issue .. 10/-

JOHN GALSWORTHY

A MODERN COMEDY
Cr. 8vo.   Green cloth

WILLIAM HEINEMANN LTD.
1929

The first issue has misprints on page 141 lines two and three; the last words of which read " beed " and " birn ."

The second issue has these words corrected to " been " and " bird."

The first edition of this book was 65,000 copies and the mistake was not discovered until approximately 40,000 copies had been printed, therefore the second issue is comparatively rarer than the first issue, but owing to the large number of copies printed for the first edition, the book has no very advanced value.

Value: First edition, either issue   ..   12/6

A SHEAF
Cr. 8vo.   Dark brown boards

WILLIAM HEINEMANN
1916

The first issue has brown top edges. Other edges uncut.

The second issue has white top edges, and foredges rough cut.

Values: First issue   ..   £5
        Second issue   ..   £3

JOHN GALSWORTHY

IN CHANCERY
Cr. 8vo
WILLIAM HEINEMANN
1920

Issued in two different shades of green cloth. The first issue is bound in bright green cloth, with gilt lettering on the spine and a gilt facsimile of the author's writing of the title of the book, across the front cover.

The second issue is bound in a much paler shade of green, but otherwise without a difference.

Values: First issue .. £3
Second issue .. 30/-

PLAYS
Green cloth. Small Square 8vo
DUCKWORTH AND CO.
1909

The first issue has continuous pagination and there are four errors in the cast for the play " Strife " viz:

Halland for Hallard
Holmwood for Homewood
  Mr. William Pilling for Mr. Drelincourt Odlam.
  Miss Ellen O'Mally for Miss Ellen O'Malley.

An errata slip is found in some copies of the first issue, drawing attention to the errors.

JOHN GALSWORTHY

There is a publishers' device in the centre of the back cover.

The second issue has " First Published, 1909 " on the verso of the title page and the publishers' device is in the lower left hand corner of the back cover. The pagination is not continuous.

The third issue has an asterisk on the spine, and " First Series " on the front cover.

The fourth issue has an asterisk on the spine, but is not lettered " First Series."

    Values: First issue .. £4
             Second issue .. £2
             Third issue .. £1
             Fourth issue .. £1

JOHN GALSWORTHY

PLAYS
FIFTH SERIES
Small 8vo. Green cloth
DUCKWORTH AND CO.
1922

The first issue does not mention " The Forsyte Saga " in the list of books on the verso of the half title. The half title pages to " Loyalties " and " Windows " are mounted on stubs.

The date of publication is given on the verso of the title page.

The second issue has no date on verso of title page, and the half titles before " Windows " and " Loyalties " have a list of the author's books on verso.

Values: First issue .. £2
Second issue .. 15/-

THE COUNTRY HOUSE
Cr. 8vo. Green cloth. Gilt lettered on spine with title in gilt across front cover.
WILLIAM HEINEMANN
1907

The first issue has the publisher's windmill device in blind in the lower right hand corner of the back cover.

The second issue has the publisher's device in the centre of the back cover.

Values: First issue .. £8
Second issue .. £4

ROBERT GRAVES
BUT STILL IT GOES ON
Cr. 8vo.   Green cloth
JONATHAN CAPE
1930

The first issue has the words "The Child She Bare" printed in italics on page 157. The second issue has not these words and the pp. 157 and 158 are mounted on a stub.

Values: First issue .. 21/-
Second issue .. 10/6

GOOD-BYE TO ALL THAT
Large Cr. 8vo.   Light red cloth, gilt
JONATHAN CAPE
1929

The first issue of this book contains a long poem by Siegfried Sassoon, which begins on page 341, line 26, with the heading "American Red Cross Hospital, No. 22, | 98–99 Lancaster Gate, W.2."

Four lines of this poem are on page 341, followed by twenty-seven lines with a two-line footnote on page 342, followed by twenty-seven lines on page 343. The second issue of the book has the poem replaced by three asterisks in V shape at the foot of page 341, and four asterisks on both pages 342 and 343, in a diamond shape in the centre of each page, which pages are devoid of text.

ROBERT GRAVES

The second edition of the book has the text, which immediately followed the poem in the first issue, or the asterisks of the second issue, brought forward, thereby causing the chapter (twenty-five) to end on page 342, instead of on page 344 as in the first edition. The first edition ends on page 448 and the second edition ends on page 446.

The first issue was withdrawn from circulation and consequently very few copies—probably less than one hundred—are in existence; the poem by Siegfried Sassoon makes the book a desirable item for collectors.

Values: First edition, first issue .. £4
First edition, second issue .. £1
Second edition .. 10/6

ON ENGLISH POETRY

Crown 8vo

WILLIAM HEINEMANN

1922

Two issues of this book have come to our notice. One is bound in yellow cloth with a black mottled design incorporating the title, and the author's name, with the publisher's windmill design on the front cover.

The second issue is bound in buff boards with paper title label on the front cover, and on the back.

Of these two issues the author writes:

"I am pretty sure that the first issue is the yellow mottled cloth because one of the six author's copies that came to me and is still in my possession is that sort.

"The design was by William Nicholson and neither he nor I liked Heinemann's interpretation of it, and the other was an improvement, on his insistence; I am pretty sure."

      Values: First issue .. £1
               Second issue .. 10/-

H. RIDER HAGGARD
MAIWA'S REVENGE

Cr. 8vo

LONGMANS GREEN AND CO.

1888

Issued in two forms, the generally accepted first issue being black cloth with red lettering on front cover and spine, decorated end papers with swan design and sixteen pages of advertisements dated June, 1888.

The second issue is bound in dark grey boards, lettering as above, plain end papers and no advertisements.

Values: First issue .. 15/-
Second issue .. 10/-

JAMES HANLEY
THE GERMAN PRISONER

Demy 8vo

PRIVATELY PRINTED

1930

The regular first edition of this book was bound in red buckram, limited to 500 copies.

A special edition for presentation only was bound in black buckram, only fifty copies being so done.

Values: First issue .. £1
Second issue .. 10/6

THOMAS HARDY
A GROUP OF NOBLE DAMES

Cr. 8vo. Light Brown cloth

OSGOOD McILVAINE
1891

The first issue has the design in gilt on the front cover, and the second issue has the design in brown. The end papers of the former should be yellow, but may be found with white end papers similar to the second issue.

Values: First issue .. £5
Second issue .. £3

TESS OF THE D'URBERVILLES

3 VOLUMES

Cr. 8vo

OSGOOD McILVAINE AND CO.
1891

The first issue has the word "road" instead of "load" on page 198 in volume three.
The edition of 1892 is often confused with that of 1891.

Values: First issue .. £25
Second issue .. £15

THOMAS HARDY

THE DYNASTS

3 VOLUMES

Crown 8vo.   Green cloth

MACMILLAN AND CO.

1903, 1906, 1908

The first issue of the first volume of this famous work was dated 1903, but its rarity is so great that it brings a high price whenever a copy is brought into the market.

The second issue of the first volume is dated 1904 at the foot of the title page, and on the verso of the title page is the imprint:— " Copyright in the United States of America."

On page XII of the preface there are thirteen lines of text, beginning with " A practical compromise may conceivably result. . . ." The last line reading :—" But on this branch of the subject the present writer is unqualified to speak."

The title page of this issue is mounted on a stub. The third issue has the date 1904 at foot of the title page, but on the verso bears the imprint:— " Copyright in the United States of America," and beneath this, " First Edition 1903. Reprinted 1904."

On page XII of the preface there are thirteen and a half lines of text beginning with :—" In respect of such plays of poesy and dream a practical compromise may conceivably result. . . ."

This passage ends with the sentence: " But with this branch of the subject we are not concerned here."

Values: First issue .. £200
Second issue .. £30
Third issue .. £10

FRANK HARRIS & LORD ALFRED DOUGLAS
NEW PREFACE TO THE LIFE AND CONFESSIONS OF OSCAR WILDE

Demy 8vo.   Black buckram

FORTUNE PRESS

1925

The first issue has a misprint on page 41, line 4; the last word " Wilde " for " Wild " (Sir Ernest Wild).   Also, the date at the foot of the letter from Frank Harris (page 55) is dated September, 1925.

The second issue has the correct name, " Wild " and the date at the foot of the letter is altered to May, 1925.

Values: First issue   ..   15/-
Second issue   ..   10/-

MAURICE HEWLETT

MRS. LANCELOT

Crown 8vo.   Blue cloth

MACMILLAN AND CO., LIMITED

1912

The first issue has gilt top edges and twelve pages of advertisements at the end of the volume.

The second issue has plain top edges and four pages of advertisements only.

Values: First issue   ..   10/-
Second issue   ..   7/6

THE SONG OF RENNY

Cr. 8vo

MACMILLAN AND CO.

1911

The first issue was bound in dark blue ribbed cloth with gilt lettering on front cover and spine, and blind decorations on front cover and spine.

The second, or remainder binding is dark blue, gilt lettering and without decorations.

Values: First issue   ..   7/6
Second issue   ..   5/-

43

LAURENCE HOUSMAN
ALL-FELLOWS

Large square Cr. 8vo

KEGAN PAUL, TRENCH, TRÜBNER AND CO
1896

The first issue is in brown buckram. On the spine is a decorative piece incorporating the word "All." Then follows the title:— Fellows | Seven | Legends | of Lower | Redemption | By | Laurence | Housman. In gilt.

The publishers' name appears at the bottom of the spine, also in gilt.

On the front cover is an elaborate gilt design. The second issue is in green cloth, gilt lettered, but does not have the design "All" on spine, the title being near the top. A dark green leaf device is placed on the spine just above the publishers' name.

Values: First issue .. £1
Second issue .. 10/-

W. H. HUDSON

GREEN MANSIONS

Cr. 8vo. Green cloth

DUCKWORTH AND CO.

1904

Of the two issues of this book, that without the publishers' design on the back cover is considered to be the first issue and the rarer. The second issue has the publishers' design which is a floral pattern incorporating a rose, intertwining branches and a fleur-de-lys, with the word " Desormais " at the bottom of the design which is in blind.

Values: First issue .. £20
Second issue .. £15

ALDOUS HUXLEY
PROPER STUDIES
Cr. 8vo. Green cloth

CHATTO AND WINDUS

1927

Although there are two forms of binding for this item, the general issue was bound in rough green cloth with top edges coloured dark green, the foredges cut and the bottom edges uncut.

Another, and presumably an advance issue only, was bound in smooth green cloth, and such copies are uncommon. The values of this item are, at present, nominal.

Value: .. 10/-

RUDYARD KIPLING
AMERICAN NOTES

Cr. 8vo.   Blue wrappers

M. J. IVERS AND CO.

NEW YORK

1891

The first issue has the address of the publishers as 86 Nassau Street, New York, and the second issue has the address 379 Pearl Street.

Values: First issue   ..   £15
    Second issue ..   £10

RUDYARD KIPLING

JUST SO STORIES FOR LITTLE CHILDREN

4to.   Red cloth

MACMILLAN AND CO., LTD.
1902

Bound in red cloth with black and white decorative figures upon both covers and on the back.

The first issue is generally accepted as that with the white decorations executed with white paint, the second being done with enamel.

Invariably, copies of the first issue are found with the lettering and decorations on the spine rubbed away. The decorations and letterings of the white paint issue are naturally whiter than those of the enamelled issue, which is dull in comparison.

Values: First issue   .. £15
        Second issue .. £10

Note: The book was first published in September, 1902, and reprinted in October, and again in November of the same year, the enamel lettering being used for both editions.

D. H. LAWRENCE

AMORES

Cr. 8vo. Dark Blue cloth

DUCKWORTH AND CO.

1916

The first issue has a sixteen page list of publishers' advertisements at the end.

The second issue has no advertisements.

Values: First issue .. £5
Second issue .. £2

MOVEMENTS IN EUROPEAN HISTORY

Cr. 8vo

HUMPHREY MILFORD

OXFORD UNIVERSITY PRESS

1921

The first issue was bound in light blue cloth; lettered on back in black.

The second issue was bound in brown cloth, black lettered as above.

Values: First issue .. £2
Second issue .. £1

D. H. LAWRENCE

ST. MAWR
Crown 8vo. Brown cloth

MARTIN SECKER

1925

The first issue is bound in dark brown cloth, top edges cut, bottom edges uncut.

The second issue is bound in a light brown cloth, top edges cut, foredges trimmed, and bottom edges uncut.

Values: First issue .. £1
Second issue .. 7/6

THE LOST GIRL
Cr. 8vo. Brown cloth

MARTIN SECKER

1920

The first issue has the text as the author originally wrote it, and the final phrase at the end of the third chapter reads: "Whether she noticed anything in the bed".

The second issue has page 268 tipped in, and the phrase above deleted.

The third issue has page 268 as part of the signature and reads the same as issue two.

Values: First issue .. £25
Second issue .. £5
Third issue .. £3

D. H. LAWRENCE

THE WHITE PEACOCK
Cr. 8vo

WILLIAM HEINEMANN

1911

The first issue binding is a dark blue-green cloth, lettered and ornamented in white on the front cover, and gilt lettering on the spine. The back cover has the publisher's device in the centre. Top and foredges cut, bottom edges uncut.

The second issue binding is without the publisher's device on the back cover.

Values: First issue .. £8
Second issue .. £4

COLONEL T. E. LAWRENCE

SEVEN PILLARS OF WISDOM

4to

1926

The two issues of this book may be called the " Complete " and the " Incomplete " issues. The correct first, or complete issue, is as follows:—SEVEN | PILLARS | OF | WISDOM | a triumph | 1926. Quarto size, morocco bindings, by various binders. Printed on hand-made paper, with uncut fore and bottom edges, top edges gilt. End papers decorated by Eric Kennington.

At the bottom of the page containing the list of illustrations (p. 19) a written note in ink in the author's hand reads " Complete Copy. I–XII–26.TES ", and on the same page is an alteration in the author's hand, the name " Roberts " being deleted and the initial " K " replacing it.

These are the chief points separating the two issues, yet it has been ascertained that many of the " Complete " copies vary in the number of the illustrations—some copies lacking plates which other " Complete " copies have and vice versa.

The " Incomplete " copies lack varying numbers of the plates and have not the author's corrections on p.19, and portions of the text have also been omitted in many cases, i.e. foreword, dedicatory poem, introduction or list of illustrations.

Values: "Complete" issue .. £300
"Incomplete" issue .. £150

FRANCIS LEDWIDGE
SONGS OF PEACE

Cr. 8vo

HERBERT JENKINS

1917

The first issue was bound in green cloth, and has two pages of publisher's advertisements at the end.

The second issue was bound in grey cloth and has a publisher's device on the back cover.

Values: First issue .. £1
Second issue .. 10/-

NOTE:—Although the issues mentioned above are presumed to be correct, the publishers, who have assisted us with great courtesy, cannot give us any definite information.

SHANE LESLIE
THE END OF A CHAPTER
Demy 8vo. Boards, canvas back

CONSTABLE AND CO.

1916

The first issue has pp. 84–85 and 199–200 as part of the collation.

The second issue has cancel leaves inserted, the original pages having been extracted and the new leaves mounted on the stubs of the old.

Values: First issue .. £1
Second issue .. 10/-

SINCLAIR LEWIS
ELMER GANTRY
Cr. 8vo. Blue cloth.

HARCOURT BRACE AND COMPANY

NEW YORK

1927

The first issue is distinguished by the letter " G " of " Gantry " on the back having the appearance of a letter " C."

The second issue has the corrected " G."

Values: First issue .. £2
Second issue .. 10/-

WILLIAM J. LOCKE
THE FORTUNATE YOUTH

Cr. 8vo

THE BODLEY HEAD

1914

The first issue was bound in red cloth, with white lettering and decorations on front cover, and gilt lettering on the spine.

Other issues are bound in green cloth or maroon cloth, these being later bindings.

Values: First issue .. 10/-
        Second issue .. 5/-

ARTHUR MACHEN
THE FORTUNATE LOVERS
Small Demy 8vo.   Royal Blue cloth

LONDON.   GEORGE REDWAY

1887

The first issue is distinguishable by the front cover decorations of a heraldic shield device in gilt within a gilt wreath, and gilt dots and floral decorations over the front cover.   Dark grey end papers.

The second issue has plain covers and white end papers.

Values: First issue .. £6
Second issue .. £2

COMPTON MACKENZIE

GUY AND PAULINE

Cr. 8vo

MARTIN SECKER

1915

The first issue was bound in strawberry coloured cloth, gilt lettered on front cover and back, and has a two-page list of the author's works at end, followed by a 16-page catalogue of publisher's announcements.
A second issue was bound in blue cloth, and lacks the publisher's advertisements.

Values: First issue .. 15/-
Second issue .. 10/-

SYLVIA AND MICHAEL

Cr. 8vo.   Black buckram

MARTIN SECKER

1919

The first issue was bound as above, lettered on back and front in green, the top edges being coloured to match the binding. Sixteen pages of advertisements at end.
The second issue was bound in blue cloth, black lettered, and the top edges plain. No advertisements at the end.

Values: First issue .. 15/-
Second issue .. 5/-

COMPTON MACKENZIE

THE SEVEN AGES OF WOMAN

Cr. 8vo. Cloth

MARTIN SECKER

1923

The first issue was bound in grey cloth, with black lettering on front cover, within a thick lined border, and lettered in black on the back. The second issue was bound in light green cloth, lettered as in the first issue, but dark green instead of black.

Values: First issue .. 10/-
Second issue .. 5/-

JOHN MASEFIELD
GALLIPOLI
Cr. 8vo

WILLIAM HEINEMANN
1916

A first issue was bound in light blue cloth, lettered on front and spine in dark blue. These copies were issued in advance for review copies, etc.
The second issue was bound in red cloth, lettered on front and back in black, and the publisher's device on back cover.

Values: First issue .. £3
Second issue .. £1

LOST ENDEAVOUR
Cr. 8vo.   Green cloth

THOMAS NELSON AND SONS
1910

The first issue was bound in light green cloth, lettered on the spine in gilt upon a white enamel panel; the publishers' name being in gilt. All edges cut. Decorated end papers. The second issue is bound in a dark green cloth, decorated in blind on front cover and on the spine; the back cover being plain. The lettering on the spine is gilt, and there is no white enamel panel. Plain end papers.

Values: First issue .. 30/-
Second issue .. 10/-

JOHN MASEFIELD

MARTIN HYDE, THE DUKE'S MESSENGER

Cr. 8vo

WELLS GARDNER, DARTON AND CO.

1910

The first issue bound in chocolate coloured cloth.
The second issues were bound in other coloured cloths, blue and green in particular.

Values: First issue .. £2
Second issue .. £1

JOHN MASEFIELD

MULTITUDE AND SOLITUDE

Cr. 8vo

GRANT RICHARDS

1909

The first issue was bound in greyish green cloth with white lettering on the front cover and on the spine. The top edges cut and the foredges trimmed. A sixteen page list of books, dated Spring, 1908, is at the end of the volume.

The second issue was bound in green cloth, white lettered on the front cover, and lettered in gilt on the spine. Top edges cut, foredges trimmed, bottom edges uncut. There is no list of books at the end.

Values: First issue .. £3
Second issue .. £1

JOHN MASEFIELD

ODTAA

Cr. 8vo. Blue cloth

WILLIAM HEINEMANN LTD.

1926

The correct first edition has eight pages of publishers' announcements at the end.
An issue is to be found without these, and was probably a colonial edition.

Values: First issue .. 15/-
Second issue .. 10/-

SEA LIFE IN NELSON'S TIME

Cr. 8vo. Dark blue cloth

METHUEN AND CO.

1905

The first issue bound as above with gilt lettering on back together with a gilt anchor device. On front cover is an elaborate design in gilt of a ship with floral border.

The first issue has forty pages of advertisements dated September, 1905, at the end.

The second issue has forty pages of advertisements dated October, 1905.

Values: First issue .. £5
Second issue .. £3

W. SOMERSET MAUGHAM
THE PAINTED VEIL
Cr. 8vo.   Dark Blue cloth

WILLIAM HEINEMANN LTD.

1925

The first issue has, on the recto of the page following the title page, one sentence which reads:—" . . . the painted veil which those who live call Life ". On page 16, line 15 of the text, the first words are " Hong Kong "; also, on page 17, line 18, the same town is mentioned, and is also mentioned throughout the book. In this first issue, the numeral " 2 " is at the right hand bottom corner of page seventeen.

The second issue has the title page and other pages mounted on a stub, and has a page of " Author's Note " inserted after the title page. The town of " Hong Kong " has been altered to that of " Tching-Yen," on all of those pages described in the first issue. Page seventeen has no numeral " 2 " at the foot.

The third issue compares with the second by the use of the word " Tching-Yen," but the numeral " 2 " again appears at the foot of page seventeen. The author's note is also included.

> Values: First issue   ..   £10
> Second issue ..   £2
> Third issue   ..   £1

GEORGE MEREDITH
SELECTED POEMS
Crown 8vo.   Brown buckram

ARCHIBALD CONSTABLE AND CO.

1897

The first edition exists in three variant issues:
1. Dark brown buckram, gilt lettered on spine " Selected | Poems. | George | Meredith | Constable | Westminster. | On the verso of pp. iv. is the imprint, Edinburgh: T. and A. Constable, Printers to her Majesty and on the verso of p. [246] is the imprint, " Printed by T. and A. Constable, Printers to her Majesty | at the Edinburgh University Press." Two pages of advertisements pp. [247–248] follow.

2. The second issue in lighter brown buckram has the lettering on the spine, " Constable | London " instead of " Constable | Westminster " and the imprint at the foot of page [246] reads: " Edinburgh: T. and A. Constable, Printers to Her Majesty " in one line.

3. Light brown buckram with " Constable | Westminster " on spine, and imprint on verso of title page: " Butler and Tanner, The Selwood Printing Works, Frome and London." This imprint also appears on verso of p. [246], and the issue has the addition

of 16 pp. of advertisements of the publishers' announcements.

Values: First issue .. £2
Second issue .. £1
Third issue .. £1

LEONARD MERRICK
WHEN LOVE FLIES OUT O' THE WINDOW

Cr. 8vo.   Cloth

C. ARTHUR PEARSON LTD.

1902

The first issue was bound in green cloth, lettered in gilt on the back with an illustrated front cover of "Love flying out of the Window."

The second issue was bound in brown cloth, gilt lettered on back; decorated with white lettering.

Values: First issue   .. £2

Second issue .. 15/-

GEORGE MOORE
ESTHER WATERS
A PLAY IN FIVE ACTS

Demy 8vo.   Boards

WILLIAM HEINEMANN

1913

The first issue was bound in grey boards, with rounded backs and paper title label on the back, with the date 1913 printed thereon.
The second issue was bound in grey-green boards, with title label on the back, which is flat.
The third issue was bound in grey boards with undated title label on the back, which is flat.

Values: First issue   .. £2
        Second issue .. £1
        Third issue   .. 10/-

IMPRESSIONS AND OPINIONS
Small Cr. 8vo.

DAVID NUTT

1891

A very rare first issue has the words, " Author of ' A Mummer's Wife ' " on the title page misprinted as " Author of ' A Humorous Wife '."
The binding of both issues is dark green cloth.

Values: First issue   .. £50
        Second issue .. £5

GEORGE MOORE

THE UNTILLED FIELD
Cr. 8vo.   Scarlet cloth
T. FISHER UNWIN
1903

The first issue was bound as above, with four pages of advertisements at the end.

Another issue is bound in brown cloth, and others in various coloured cloths bear the imprint on the title, and at the bottom of the spine, of George Bell and Sons.

Values: First issue .. £3
Second issue .. 10/-

A. E. NEWTON

THIS BOOK-COLLECTING GAME

Demy 8vo.   Canvas Cloth

GEORGE ROUTLEDGE AND SONS
1930

The first issue was withdrawn because of a reference to a well known London bookseller on page 195.

The second issue does not mention the name of this firm and the page is mounted on a stub.

Values : First issue .. 25/-
Second issue .. 15/-

LIAM O'FLAHERTY
TWO YEARS

Cr. 8vo.   Blue cloth

JONATHAN CAPE
1930

This book has two issues of the dust wrapper. The first has the price 10/6d. net, in lower corner of the front inside flap.

The second issue has the price torn away and the price of 7/6d. printed below the last line of text on the inside flap.

Values: First issue   .. 15/-
Second issue   .. 10/-

EDEN PHILLPOTTS
THE PORTREEVE

Cr. 8vo.   Red cloth

METHUEN AND CO.
1906

The first issue has forty pages of advertisements at the end of the volume, dated, November 1905.

Later issues have advertisements dated January 1906

Values: First issue .. £1

Second issue .. 10/-

J. B. PRIESTLEY
THE GOOD COMPANIONS
Demy 8vo.   Blue cloth

LONDON

WILLIAM HEINEMANN

1929

There are three issues of this book, and the second is the rarest, and may be distinguished by the blank space in line 17, page 66. This is generally accepted to be the second issue. The first and third issues have this space filled with the word "ordinary," and the first issue is difficult to compare with the third except that in some copies, the type is not quite even.

During the printing, the omission was discovered and rectified, but it is difficult to say with any certainty which is the first or the third issue, but we can say that the second, possessing the "point" of the missing word, and being rarer, will be considered the most desirable issue by collectors.

Values: First and third issues   .. £4

Second issue   .. £5

ANNE DOUGLAS SEDGWICK

ANNE DOUGLAS SEDGWICK

THE LITTLE FRENCH GIRL

Cr. 8vo.   Green cloth

CONSTABLE AND CO., LTD.

1924

A rare first issue of probably less than twenty copies of this book exists with the title printed as " A Little French Girl " on the front cover and on the back.

In the second issue the correct title of " The Little French Girl" appears.

Values: First issue   ..   £2
Second issue   ..   15/-

G. BERNARD SHAW
THE QUINTESSENCE OF IBSENISM

Cr. 8vo.   Green cloth

CONSTABLE AND CO.

1913

This edition with the new preface dated 1913 is to be found in two issues; the first with gilt lettering on spine, and the second with black lettering.

Values: First issue .. 10/-

Second issue .. 5/-

OSBERT SITWELL
TRIPLE FUGUE

Cr. 8vo.   Boards.   Cloth back

GRANT RICHARDS

1924

The first issue is bound in bright red boards, decorated with gilt crescents on the front and back covers. A paper title label with black open letter type is affixed to the cloth back. An extra title label is attached to one of the back end papers.

The second issue is bound in red cloth, plain sides; the title and the author's name, together with that of the publisher, is blocked in gilt on the back strip.

Values: First issue   ..   30/-
Second issue   ..   15/-

R. L. STEVENSON

ISLAND NIGHTS' ENTERTAINMENTS

Small Demy 8vo.   Cloth boards

CASSELL AND COMPANY

1893

Issued in various coloured bindings, to which no issue can be definitely assigned, but the first issue of the book can be discovered by the list of the author's works before the half title. In this list, the earliest copies have the price of the book altered in ink from 5/- to 6/-, and the sixteen pages of advertisements at the end of the volume are dated "7 G—3.93".

The later issue has the sixteen pages of advertisements dated "7G—4.93".

Values: First issue   .. £2

Second issue .. £1

J. A. SYMONDS
IN THE KEY OF THE BLUE
Cr. 8vo.   Cloth

MACMILLAN AND CO.

1893

The first issue is bound in light blue cloth, and the second issue is bound in cream cloth, lettered in gold. Very few copies of the first issue exist, such copies having been withheld from circulation owing to the designer (Mr. Charles Ricketts) objecting to the blue colour.

Values: First issue .. £5
Second issue .. £2

ARTHUR SYMONS
AN INTRODUCTION TO THE STUDY OF BROWNING

Small Cr. 8vo.   Dark green cloth

CASSELL AND COMPANY, LIMITED
1886

Although a copy of this book is recorded by Viscount Esher, with the advertisements dated September, the bibliography gives the date of the first issue of the catalogue as " 5.G.10.86," we have noted a copy with the advertisements dated " 5.G.7.87," but can find no textual changes.

There are no half titles to either issue.

Values: First issue .. 25/-

Second issue .. £1

ARTHUR SYMONS

THE TOY CART

Cr. 8vo.   Brown boards

MAUNSEL AND COMPANY

1919

The first issue is bound in dark brown boards, with canvas back, and a paper label with title and author's name affixed to the back. Top edges cut, fore and bottom edges uncut. The second issue is bound in light grey brown boards, linen back, paper label as above. All edges uncut.

Values: First issue   ..   12/6
        Second issue ..   5/-

H. M. TOMLINSON

TIDEMARKS

Demy 8vo. Brown cloth

CASSELL AND COMPANY

1924

There are two issues of this book, and the issue which is generally accepted as the first is that with the gilt device of a palm tree upon the spine.

The second issue has not this device.

Values: First issue .. £4

Second issue .. £3

ℰDGAR WALLACE
THE FOUR JUST MEN
Cr. 8vo.   Yellow cloth

THE TALLIS PRESS
1905

It is important that the first edition of this book must contain the entry form for the Solution competition, which follows page 224, otherwise the first edition is incomplete.

Value .. £1

HUGH WALPOLE

FORTITUDE

Cr. 8vo.   Red cloth

MARTIN SECKER
1913

The first issue has advertisements at the end dated January 1913. Scarlet top edges.

The second issue has advertisements dated Spring 1913. Brown top edges.

Values: First issue   ..   £4
Second issue   ..   £3

THE DARK FOREST

Cr. 8vo

MARTIN SECKER
1916

The first issue is bound in black buckram, lettered on back, and on the front covers in red.   All edges uncut.

The second issue is bound in bright red buckram, with white grey lettering. Top edges red.

Values: First issue   ..   £3
Second issue   ..   £1

H. G. WELLS
MEN LIKE GODS
Cr. 8vo. Green cloth

CASSELL AND COMPANY
1923

The first issue was bound in green cloth, with gilt lettering on the back, and blind lettering on the front cover. Top and foredges cut, bottom edges uncut.

The second issue has the bottom edges cut, and the lettering of the name " Cassell " on the bottom of the spine is in blind instead of gilt.

Values: First issue .. 30/-
Second issue .. 7/6

NEW WORLDS FOR OLD
Cr. 8vo. Red cloth, gilt lettered

ARCHIBALD CONSTABLE AND CO.
1908

The first issue has the fore and lower edges uncut.

The second issue has the top edges trimmed, the other edges being uncut.

Values: First issue .. £2
Second issue .. £1

THE FOOD OF THE GODS
AND
HOW IT CAME TO EARTH

Cr. 8vo. Sage Green cloth

MACMILLAN AND CO., LIMITED

1904

The first issue has eighteen pages of publishers' advertisements at the end, dated 20/7/04.

The second issue has eighteen pages of publishers' advertisements at the end, dated 20/9/04; the first two pages being unnumbered.

Values: First issue .. £2
Second issue .. £1

Note. Copies of both issues exist with the top edges plain, or gilt.

THE SECRET PLACES OF THE HEART

Cr. 8vo. Cloth

CASSELL AND CO., LTD.

1922

The first issue is bound in dark green cloth, gilt lettered on back, and lettered in blind on front cover with decorations in blind on back and front covers. On the verso of the title page is printed, " First published 1922."

The second issue is bound in light green cloth, no lettering on front cover, lettered in black on the back strip. A publishers' device of a feminine artist appears on the title page, and the verso is lettered " First published, May 1922," and at the foot of the title page is " Printed in Great Britain."

Values: First issue .. £1
Second issue .. 7/6

THE WAR OF THE WORLDS

Cr. 8vo.   Grey cloth

LONDON

WILLIAM HEINEMANN

1898

The first issue has sixteen pages of publisher's advertisements at the end, of " Mr. William Heinemann's Autumn Announcements " dated MDCCCXCVII.

The second issue lacks the advertisements.

Values: First issue .. £2
Second issue .. £1

SIZES OF BOOKS.

For the convenience of readers of this book this table gives the usual sizes of bound books.

Crown 16mo.	$5 \times 3\frac{3}{4}$
Demy 16mo.	$5\frac{5}{8} \times 4\frac{3}{8}$
Royal 16mo.	$6\frac{1}{2} \times 5$
Fcap 8vo.	$6\frac{3}{4} \times 4\frac{1}{4}$
Crown 8vo.	$7\frac{1}{2} \times 5$
Fcap 4to.	$8\frac{1}{2} \times 6\frac{3}{4}$
Demy 8vo.	$8\frac{3}{4} \times 5\frac{5}{8}$
Med. 8vo.	$9\frac{1}{2} \times 6$
Crown 4to.	$10 \times 7\frac{1}{2}$
Royal 8vo.	$10 \times 6\frac{1}{4}$
S. Royal 8vo.	$10\frac{1}{4} \times 6\frac{7}{8}$
Imp. 8vo.	$11 \times 7\frac{1}{2}$
Demy 4to.	$11\frac{1}{4} \times 8\frac{3}{4}$
Med. 4to.	$12 \times 9\frac{1}{2}$
Royal 4to.	$12\frac{1}{2} \times 10$
S. Royal 4to.	$13\frac{3}{4} \times 10\frac{1}{4}$
Imp. 4to.	15×11
Demy folio	$17\frac{1}{2} \times 11\frac{1}{4}$
Med. folio	$19 \times 12\frac{1}{2}$
Royal folio	$20 \times 12\frac{1}{2}$

INDEX

AUTHOR	TITLE	PAGE
Abercrombie (Lascelles)	Emblems of Love	1
Baring (Maurice)	Lost Diaries	2
Barrie (J. M.)	An Edinburgh Eleven	3
Barrie (J. M.)	Shall we join the Ladies?	4
Bates (H. E.)	Catherine Foster	5
Beerbohm (Max)	Seven Men	6
Bennett (Arnold)	A Man from the North	7
Bennett (Arnold)	Journalism for Women	7
Birrell (Augustine)	Obiter Dicta	8
Bone (David)	Merchantmen-at-Arms	9
Brooke (Rupert)	Letters from America	10
Burke (Thomas)	Whispering Windows	11
Campbell (Roy)	Adamastor	12
Chesterton (G. K.)	The Ball and the Cross	13
Chesterton (G. K.)	Manalive	13
Chesterton (G. K.)	Orthodoxy	14
Coppard (A. E.)	Clorinda Walks in Heaven	15
Coppard (A. E.)	Pink Furniture	15 & 16
Coppard (A. E.)	The Black Dog	17 & 18
Crockett (S. R.)	Lads' Love	19
Davidson (John)	Earl Lavender	20
De la Mare (Walter)	Memoirs of a Midget	21
De la Mare (Walter)	The Three Mulla Mulgars	22
Douglas (Norman)	Old Calabria	23
Dowson (Ernest)	La Fille aux Yeux d'Or	24
Doyle (A. Conan)	The Doings of Raffle Haw	25
Drinkwater (John)	Cromwell and Other Poems	26
Drinkwater (John)	Poems of Men and Hours	26
Dunsany (Lord)	Fifty Poems	27
Flecker (James Elroy)	Forty Two Poems	28
Flecker (James Elroy)	Selected Poems	28
Freeman (John)	The Grove and Other Poems	29
Galsworthy (John)	A Modern Comedy	30
Galsworthy (John)	A Sheaf	30
Galsworthy (John)	In Chancery	31
Galsworthy (John)	Plays	31 & 32
Galsworthy (John)	Plays (Fifth Series)	33
Galsworthy (John)	The Country House	33
Graves (Robert)	But Still It Goes On	34

INDEX

AUTHOR	TITLE	PAGE
Graves (Robert)	Good-bye to all That	34 & 35
Graves (Robert)	On English Poetry	35 & 36
Haggard (H. Rider)	Maiwa's Revenge	37
Hanley (James)	The German Prisoner	38
Hardy (Thomas)	A Group of Noble Dames	39
Hardy (Thomas)	Tess of the D'Urbervilles	39
Hardy (Thomas)	The Dynasts	40 & 41
Harris (Frank)	New Preface to The Life and Confessions of Oscar Wilde	42
Hewlett (Maurice)	Mrs. Lancelot	43
Hewlett (Maurice)	The Song of Renny	43
Housman (Laurence)	All-Fellows	44
Hudson (W. H.)	Green Mansions	45
Huxley (Aldous)	Proper Studies	46
Kipling (Rudyard)	American Notes	47
Kipling (Rudyard)	Just So Stories for Little Children	48
Lawrence (D. H.)	Amores	49
Lawrence (D. H.)	Movements in European History	49
Lawrence (D. H.)	St. Mawr	50
Lawrence (D. H.)	The Lost Girl	50
Lawrence (D. H.)	The White Peacock	51
Lawrence (Colonel)	Seven Pillars of Wisdom	52 & 53
Ledwidge (Francis)	Songs of Peace	54
Leslie (Shane)	The End of a Chapter	55
Lewis (Sinclair)	Elmer Gantry	56
Locke (William J.)	The Fortunate Youth	57
Machen (Arthur)	The Fortunate Lovers	58
Mackenzie (Compton)	Guy and Pauline	59
Mackenzie (Compton)	Sylvia and Michael	59
Mackenzie (Compton)	The Seven Ages of Woman	60
Masefield (John)	Gallipoli	61
Masefield (John)	Lost Endeavour	61
Masefield (John)	Martin Hyde	62
Masefield (John)	Multitude and Solitude	63
Masefield (John)	Odtaa	64
Masefield (John)	Sea Life in Nelson's Time	64
Maugham (Somerset)	The Painted Veil	65
Meredith (George)	Selected Poems	66 & 67
Merrick (Leonard)	When Love Flies Out o' the Window	68
Moore (George)	Esther Waters	69
Moore (George)	Impressions and Opinions	69
Moore (George)	The Untilled Field	70
Newton (A. E.)	This Book Collecting Game	71
O'Flaherty (Liam)	Two Years	72

INDEX

AUTHOR	TITLE	PAGE
Phillpotts (Eden)	The Portreeve	73
Priestley (J. B.)	The Good Companions	74
Sedgwick (Anne Douglas)	The Little French Girl	75
Shaw (G. Bernard)	The Quintessence of Ibsenism	76
Sitwell (Osbert)	Triple Fugue	77
Stevenson (R. L.)	Island Nights' Entertainments	78
Symonds (J. A.)	In the Key of the Blue	79
Symons (Arthur)	An Introduction to the Study of Browning	80
Symons (Arthur)	The Toy Cart	81
Tomlinson (H. M.)	Tidemarks	82
Wallace (Edgar)	The Four Just Men	83
Walpole (Hugh)	Fortitude	84
Walpole (Hugh)	The Dark Forest	84
Wells (H. G.)	Men Like Gods	85
Wells (H. G.)	New Worlds for Old	85
Wells (H. G.)	The Food of the Gods	86
Wells (H. G.)	The Secret Places of the Heart	86
Wells (H. G.)	The War of the Worlds	87

MADE AND PRINTED IN GREAT BRITAIN BY PURNELL AND SONS
PAULTON (SOMERSET) AND LONDON